T0319194

Epistle
To Afrophobic South Africa

Nkwazi N. Mhango

Langaa Research & Publishing CIG
Mankon, Bamenda

Publisher:

Langaa RPCIG
Langaa Research & Publishing Common Initiative Group
P.O. Box 902 Mankon
Bamenda
North West Region
Cameroon
Langaagrp@gmail.com
www.langaa-rpcig.net

Distributed in and outside N. America by African Books Collective
orders@africanbookscollective.com
www.africanbookscollective.com

ISBN-10: 9956-553-48-4

ISBN-13: 978-9956-553-48-8

© Nkwazi N. Mhango 2023

All rights reserved.
No part of this book may be reproduced or transmitted in any form or by
any means, mechanical or electronic, including photocopying and
recording, or be stored in any information storage or retrieval system,
without written permission from the publisher

Acknowledgements

My wife Nesaa, I thank you so kindly
You have always stood with me in thick and thin
You donated many ideas and improved this volume
I thank you wholeheartedly
No way can deliver my thanks adequately
Nonetheless, please know that you contributed in this hugely
Our kids Ng'ani, Nkuzi, and Nkwazi Jr also had a role to play
You kept me checked asking what was in the pipeline
You asked many crucial questions about this quandary

My friend and Mentor Mzee Pius Msekwa wherever you are
You deserve many thanks for the challenge and
encouragement
I still remember your wittiness
You kept me burning the night oil inscribing this poesy
You always encouraged me to aim higher and higher
Thanks, Musilanga original though I am your *Omukama*
Yes, in our humour word I am
And you know that I truly I am

Table of Contents

Acknowledgments iii

Epistle 1

Foreign Africans in Africa! 11

Berlin-cloned Nations 23

Why Acting Like Simians? 37

What Is the Issue? 45

South African Economy 49

Is Africa Becoming A Laughingstock .... Error!
Bookmark not defined.

Decolonise Your Country 57

How Can You Easily Forget? 63

Did You Know? 69

What A Pity! 73

Mungu Twaomba 83

Acknowledgements

Preface

Foreword

Dedication

Epistle

This epistle is for South Africa and Africa
Yes, it is the letter from Africa to Africa and in particularly
to South Africa
It is for South Africa and about Africa
It addresses a very disturbing trend revolving around
Afrophobia
The unfounded fear of Africa by Africans
It is double-edged and more of a typical replica
Of what Africa and Africans need to do to avoid pointless
self-destruction
This is the epistle that tells it as it is and to the face of it
It is serious but not in any form a gambit
This epistle will not spare anybody
Thus, the world must carefully read this epistle
Thus, dear brother and sister
Please read this epistle
It is for everybody
Naked truth in it will set you free
Take it even if you abhor it

There is one crucial thing this epistle seeks to toggle
Yes, it is nothing but collective flapdoodle
With egotism one lives in a false bubble
About this we don't need to haggle or joggle
Instead, we need to ferociously face racialism
Although this sometimes minds it may boggle
For me, there is no any niggle
No giggle
I am not available for anybody to diddle
We need to get the solution to the problem
No way we can get the solution
It is only possible in oblivion
Without truly doing justice

We need true justice
But not the justice of the jungle
Africa needs to stand as one
No chance to play the second fiddle
Nobody is supposed or left to niggle

I am writing this masterpiece with confidence
I am confident that all will work on the matter
Africa needs to move forward from colonial residues
For, it has lost a lot to this madness
Africans need to wake up and fight for justice for all
We need to fight for equality for all
Africans need to stand up and fight the stinking divisions
Yes, colonial divisions are the cause of this all
More importantly, Africans need to stand together
For, they have always suffered together
This Afrophobia South Africans are enacting will affect
them together

I humbly thus, invite all thinkers wherever they are
Where are you African sages
Come all people of all ages
Get out of your mental cages
We no longer are savages
Together, let us solve this conundrum
Unitedly, let us fight for our decorum

Where are you the custodians of our knowledge?
Yes, I mean our noble traditional knowledge
I call upon all griots and patriots in African modes
Come join me to take South Africa's Afrophobic malady
on
South Africa badly and bigly needs us to help it out of this
idiocy
If there is anything that South Africa now needs from us is
nothing but lucidness

Collective sanity seems to lack in this so-called Rainbow
populace
Let us, as humans, stand firm and help this diseased nation
To do it, I thus, write this exclusive and special epistle to
all nations
I warn all xenophobes, *xenoafrophobes* and the like
They must rethink their take
Africa doesn't need their fake and toxic nationalism
It is tired of this collective barbarism
Africa needs lucid and realistic collectivism
As it was before it succumbed to colonialism

Dear South African Brothers and Sisters
Everybody would like to see South Africa out of this
daggle
I would like to see Africans——who in life——have to
snuggle
I would like to actualise our collaborative and cooperative
struggle
When will Africa get out of this bogle?
Will it do so through this collective niggle?
Wherein some are looking at each other like puggles
Where everybody foreign is but a doomed muggle
While this is ongoing, quislings see no boondoggle
The ones I see in the upper echelons of power

This epistle revolves around intermittent Afrophobic
attacks
Wherein people attack each other like sharks
Africa is the continent of people but not of sharks
Let me urge you to stop this craze and haze of demeanour
It is built on and the result of the dehumanisation of
others by their brethren
Such a comportment is more than one can define
I say this with all of my valour
Guys, we have lost our glamour

Guys, even animals do not *de-animalize* others the way
humans dehumanise others
Animals have no morality or complicated nature like
humans
Why's South Africa allowed itself to be defined by such
collective savagery?
What will South Africa get from this jiggery piggery cum
skulduggery
Where has the sanity that Mandela and others brought
gone?
Is this what the rest of Africa sacrificed for really?
Why have South Africans easily forgotten?

Dear South Africans
You are now asininely and blindly killing Zimbabweans
You are torturing Kenyans and Guineans
Soullessly, you are hunting them like muskrats
Despite them being your kin, you treat them like mere rats
What makes this worse, this is openly and collectively
done in their own continent
You shamelessly call them invaders as if they are
How can they be invaders in their continent?
Look at Europeans
They are now uniting their continent
Naturally, Zimbabweans are your artificial neighbours
You used to be one and united as humans
Ugh! Do you know how much Zimbabwe lost for your
cause?
If you don't, please revert to your history just now
Knowing this will free you from this collective folly
You truly will see that what you are now doing is gory and
immoral
Zimbabwe had its independence delayed because of you
Is this the way any sane people can reciprocate really?
Where did the sense of the nation go?
Shall things change in South Africa, where will you go?

He who burns down his house knows why ashes cost a
fortune
Please avert this self-inflicted misfortune

Dear visionless South Africans
You are heartlessly torturing and killing Mozambicans
Ironically, they are the ones you used to run to those days
When apartheid was at its heydays
Have you easily and quickly forgotten!
They faithfully stood by you in your dark days
When apartheid was destroying you, they stood by and
with you
Why has South Africa refused to learn from apartheid?
Apartheid by whites or blacks will always be apartheid
Why are you shamelessly replicating the same iniquity?
Why are you perfecting the same inanity?
Can't you see this criminality!
Those who refuse to learn from history are always
doomed
This becomes worse, especially when victims become
offenders

Dear South Africans
Mozambican lost its first President because of you
Had the icon Samora Machel not fearlessly fought for you
He would be among us living his life today
However, what would this do for him?
Life of betraying others was not for him
His was to die like a hero than living like a coward
For your freedom, Samora willingly, at his prime, died
Though he knew what would happen to him
For the love of a united Africa, he sacrificed everything to
see you free
Now that you are free, this sacrifice has become a non-
issue!
This makes you unfree as a people

If you were truly free as a people
You would not be killing his people!
The very people with whom you used to snuggle
All of the sudden have become the trolls!

Dear South Africans
I say this with much wretchedness
I didn't expect such collective foolhardiness
You're now ruthlessly and barefacedly killing Tanzanians
You are rounding Nigerians
What a collective shame!
There is no other name I can assign to this infamy
I shall always call this a shame of shames
Aren't the same that offered a shelter during the struggles
for liberation?
Have you easily and quickly forgotten Tanzania was the
hub of liberation?
Yes, it was the hub of liberation struggles in the Southern
Africa
And this exposed Tanzania to sabotage from Western
powers
Have you easily forgotten the Frontline States whose
headquarters were Dar?
Wow! This is not sad but also heretical
Have you forgotten how Tanzania sacrificed its economy
for you?
Have you forgotten how Tanzania generously and
unconditionally provided refuge to you!
Go to Mazimbu or Solomon Mahlangu camp
Remember there how you used to romp
Remember how most of Africa sacrificed much for you
Is this the way you can generously pay?
Is this the way you can hail Africa's contribution to you!

Dear South Africans
You are now cold-bloodedly killing Zambians

You blindly hate Namibians
Aren't they your next neighbours in this colonial setting?
Didn't they offer their land to you to use unconditionally?
For supporting you, didn't they suffer terribly?
Haven't they been good neighbours to you?
Who chooses a neighbour?
Mzee Kenneth Kaunda, with anger and dismay, must be
sobbing
Sam Nujoma must be regretting
For the sacrifices they made on the expenses of their
people
They must be regretting their love of unity and freedom
Is this what they sacrificed everything for
Wasn't Lusaka your second home as Windhoek was?
Wow! What an unthankful nation that is!
Have you easily forgotten!

Dear Brothers and Sisters
Like a wake of vultures, you are now attacking others
You rob whomever you come across like scavengers
You don't discern who is culpable or innocent
To you, being a foreigner warrants the slaughters
Yet, some of you see this as justice!
Bloviating aside, what type of justice is this?
Such injustices will never make you safer
Everything will come a cropper
Stop Afrophobia before it turns against you
Remember how apartheid turned against itself
It cannibalised itself before its death
Where is it now?

Dear Brothers and Sisters
Today you are brutally mistreating and killing Angolans
You wrongly think they are a danger to your otherworldly
chic lives
Without peace, how will you enjoy such lives?

You are, as well, butchering Malawians
What will you do shall they tomorrow turn against you in
the same manner?
What will you do shall they learn this jungle justice from
you?
What sins did they commit so as to deserve such
mistreatments?
Their original sin is nothing but helping you
Their mistake is to unconditionally support your liberation

The killings of other Africans will not solve your problems
Instead, it will exacerbate them
The solutions are simple and clear
Go after your true enemies whoever they are
Seek them wherever they are
You know them though you are afraid of them
Go to the government and ask it who you enemies are

Dear only and true but blind BRETHREN
Some whinge that foreigners take their ladies
Yes, they may if you maltreat them as it has been the
practices
Rape has increased countrywide
Who want to live in such a world?
Love seeks safety and peace besides being a personal
choice
Instead of complaining just ask yourselves
Why this happening and what are the causes
Getting down to the bottom of this is the only solution
Respect your women
Respect your girls
Stop raping them
Stop beating them
Stop systemic rape that is rampant in South Africa
Let South Africa be defined by peace but not criminality as
it currently is

Stop violence in the street and at home
Your ladies must feel safe wherever they are
Try this everything will change
Faith will return and love will resume
Your ancestors did not do this
Apartheid made you do this
Now that apartheid is long gone
It is upon you to change and device the destiny of your
nation

Foreign Africans in Africa!

Dear Brothers and Sisters wherever you may be
Can you clearly and loudly hear me?
My sound is clear not a bong
If it were a drum, it is a bongo
If you do, please listen to me
Can you as well educate me?
Educate me wherever you think I have gone wrong
What I have gotten wrong
Never stop so me telling

I have a solution to a problem emanating from
Afrophobia
Listen to the nuggets of wisdom I hold dear
In ameliorating your situation, please, seriously, make this
germane
I am speaking calmly without any diatribe
I want you to learn but not on me to take a jibe
If we can't learn from each other, who will teach us?
How can we then learn from each while we discriminate
against each other?
If we cannot listen to each other, who'll listen to us?
How can we listen while we are killing each other?
How can we loved if we hate one another?
Let us reason together
Let's face it together
Afrophobia needs to stop

Dear African brothers and sisters
We need to collectively concur
To do so we must firstly avoid rancour
We are the ones who have to solve our problems
I call upon you who call yourselves South Africans
Are you realistically South Africans?

Who made you South Africans?
Who are South Africans as opposed to other Africans?
To me, Africans are Africans
Regardless of what they pride themselves about as their
nations
I'm writing this after witnessing many ruckuses claiming
many innocent lives
It shocks and bemoans to see such silliness committed by
Africans against Africans
Yes, I am writing this because of fracas we often evidence
in South Africa like volcanic eruptions they are always up and
down
As sober as I am, I can see what you miss
This epistle is specifically written to South Africans
Sane and otherwise South Africans
Africans who think they are not Africans
While even birds know they are but Africans

Dear Everybody
For the first time in my life, I must admit
I did not expect to evidence such a gambit
I heard of foreigners who happen to be Africans in Africa!
Up until now, surely, I cannot stomach it let alone
understanding it
How can Africans be foreigners anywhere in Africa?
How'll we call real foreigners who crossed seas to come to
Africa?
How'll we call the remnants of colonialism?
How'll we treat those who brought their toxic isms to
Africa?
The very isms that divide Africa
How'll you define those who enhanced colonialism to
penetrate Africa?
Missionaries do hear me clearly
I have not forgotten your role
The one that you played in paving way for colonialism

How'll we call those who are now betraying Africa?
How'll you define all those robbing you under all sorts of
isms?

If Africans are foreigners in Africa, who is an African?
To whom does Africa truly belong without Africans?
What's wrong in this crazy hodgepodge?
I am asking this seriously in order to comprehend
When did Africans become foreigners in their land?
Are we such imbeciles
How, can we be such batty?

Dear South Africans
You call other Africans *amakwerekwere* or foreigners
First of all, this is but a genocidal language
Those who committed it started with such toxic languages
Stop tagging people
Can Africans be foreigners in Africa!
What a dirty and wrong taxonomy!
Do you know the effects of such infamy?
What'll they be called in the Americas or Europe?
How will they be treated in Guadeloupe?
Isn't this moniker colonialism in itself?
Isn't this stinking self-hate and mental cuff?
Try to remember your true history please
Do you remember that those you call foreigners?
They did not call you foreigners when you were exiled
Instead, with both hands, they had you acclaimed
In their homes you were settled
In their countries you were accepted
Everything they were able to provide they offered
Whole heartedly you blended and later succeeded
Mandela once travelled on a Tanzanian passport
And this was alright
For Africa is a one entity
Tanzania recognised human intersubjectivity

So, too it understood the interconnectivity of our
survivability
We need to revive our livability, interminability and
unanimity
Let us rekindle the heart of our organic communality
Why not if at all Africa is one?
You shamelessly call the so-called foreigners from Africa
amakwerekwere
Let's face it; were you called so in the land of Nyerere?
Were you referred to as that in the country of Khama and
Ketumile?
Weren't you acclaimed in the land of Machel?
Go ask Mbeki, Zuma and Motlanthe
They know the Truth

How'll you feel shall Khoikhoi refer to you as
amakwerekwere?
Why can't you behave like Japanese mushrooms known as
matsutake
These guys can coexist with anything provided they all
survive
Wherever you put them, they will be well and alive
For, they know as the entire Africa knows that originally
your ancestry is somewhere
Yes, somewhere in the Congo forests you originated at the
time of yore
Even many varieties of animals in South Africa came from
somewhere
Do you call animals from Africa *amakwerekwere*
Did you call the Gupta robbers *amakwerekwere?*
Did you call the engineers of the state capture
amakwerekwere?
Do you call drinking water that comes from neighbouring
amakwerekwere?
Do you call Boers *amakwerekwere* jibber-jabber?

Why is it that animals are free to roam in Africa but not
Africans?
Are animals smarter than humans?
Don't animals move freely in Africa while people don't?
Do you ask them to carry passports?
Do they buy visas to roam in their Africa?
Don't animals own their parks while paupers own
nonentity?
Aren't these important things for the country to ponder
on?
These are the things you need to question
Ask your rulers such a foundation

South Africa needs true and practical liberation
Whole, realistic and paradigmatic one
Yes, true liberation from itself and its self-inflicted agony
Accordingly, South Africa badly needs full and meaningful
salvation
This time South Africa doesn't need Jesus or religions to
bring the said salvation
Jesus and religions were there when South Africa was
colonised
Religions were used in the colonisation of Africa
Our beliefs and knowledge were felled and turned us into
automata
These colonisers uplifted their dirty dogmata
Under foreign religions we became naturally original
sinners
Europeans were and still are the original sinners
They are the ones who sold Africans to slavery
They are the one that were involved in thievery
They are the ones that invented racism
They crafted colonialism
They imposed on us capitalism
Exploitation
Degradation

Dehumanisation
Division
The list goes on and on

Dear Brothers and Sisters
Seriously beware of modern religions
They have nothing to offer except pains
They practically participated in and preached the
colonisation of Africa
To make matters worse
They called their criminality civilisation as if it were
Mandela tried by building the foundations that now are
being demolished
Mandela's work is now forgotten; and verily, he is
mindlessly betrayed
Those he fought to liberate are now destroying what he's
ready to die for
What he lived and was ready to die for has become futile
His hope and sweat have become null
We verily need to save South Africa from itself

Africans need to save themselves from themselves
Though they are made to believe Jesus can save them
Where was he when they were colonised?
Didn't missionaries spread colonialism?
Have we ever held them accountable?
Weren't they in the same bed with colonial governments?
Wasn't apartheid preached by using the very same Bible?
Wasn't the Quran around when African were enslaved?
Why didn't they stop this puerility?

Dear Brothers and Sisters
Now, you know everything clearly
It is upon you to face the reality and think thoughtfully
Nobody will save Africa but Africans themselves
Nobody will save South Africans but Africans likewise

It is time for Africans to become wise
Stand up and emancipate yourselves
Forget about donors and Godfathers
There is no way your former colonial masters can become
your uncles
Theirs always is to keep you in the debacle if not in
manacles
Forget about their lures of happiness and miracles
Forget their fake promises made in their religions
True happiness is in your missions
The missions upon your true liberation

Dear African brothers and sisters
When Rwanda was destroying itself, foreign religions were
there
They are the same that preached divisions
Yes, the ones that created the bedlam Africa is in today
The stakes are always high
Some became parts and parcels of the carnage
Somalia today is bleeding in the hands of the same
pedigree
A religion is there adding more fire
Nigeria is bleeding to death
The CAR is wringing to death
As they enslaved and robbed you, religions will be there
Theirs is not to liberate you, instead, they are there to
divide you
Therefore, it is upon you and squarely on you
True liberation of Africa will always be on your shoulders

Dear Brothers and Sisters
Remember the words retired Archbishop Tutu once said
He said that when white men came brought just a Bible
They told you to close your eyes; and indeed, you did
When you opened your eyes, the Bible was in your hands!

They had your land in their hands
In this, you weren't alone; the entire Africa faced the same
It suffered and still suffers heavily in God's *name*
Religion became a game changer
Under it, Africa became a great loser
We lost our names and assumed theirs
They butchered our ways and imposed theirs
They left us confused as we are nowadays

Dear Victims
I would love to awaken your whims and vims
We need to face and unearth colonial schemes
Again, who will fulfill this onus?
If at all, we all are accomplices
Let us face it openly and realistically
Does Africa have anything to offer to South Africa really?
How, while the same Afrophobia is replicated in the
backdoor?
How can we if we heartlessly are butchering our
neighbours next-door?
How can we, while we mindlessly have ignored our
ancestral spoor?
Why aren't all African countries ready to let go their
borders?
Why are they forcing their *neighbours* to carry passports?
Can a simian laugh at another's butt and be sane?
Beasts will never be responsible for their actions, but
humans always will
Why should humans behave destructively really?

Admittedly, it is sad and painful to say albeit
Who would in a clear mind dare to consider even
distantly?
Who would think the country of Mandela would go to
pye-dogs?
Who would expect before long

That the country of Mandela is on fire?
Everything has gone haywire
Africa is in a quagmire
What was conceived as a rainbow nation is now a vampire
Who'd dare and still stand among thinkers and leaders
Let us face it truthfully and openly
Where is the Rainbow Nation currently?

South Africa has one moniker now
It is still a Nation of the rainbow?
Instead, it isn't the country that bigotry and ignorance
have choked?
The country that has sacrificed its true history
A colonial tool that any goon can use to wreak havoc
This reminds me of the story of the rogue
The gullible monkey that laughed at another
When this simian saw the back of another
Instead of thinking of how it looks like
It burst into laughter
In the end, it found it was laughing at itself

How do you conceptualise the sin of bigotry?
How do you call a black man who persecutes another?
Is there any mental disease bigger than this dishonour?
Tell me please, if you can
Those who are ready to stomach this sin please come
forth
Fearlessly come please and educate me
For, it behoves me to ask without any feeling of indignity
Why Africans have embraced unfamiliarity so as to
abandon the reality?
Bear with me please if you honestly have the guts
This is what I call the marriage between conceit and
unfamiliarity

Phew! Ignorance and arrogance treated as knowledge
while they are not
Arrogance and ignorance have bred hatred and bigotry
A black man is torching a black man on the vivid daylight!
If you ask why and what is the root cause of such incivility
A naïve answer is 'because he or she is a foreigner in my
country'
May I humbly ask whose country?
Let me assume that this is your country!
If I may ask again which country?
Do you know what you call your country is the creation of
your tyrants?
Who created the current African countries if we face it?
Isn't it the Berlin Conference that enacted colonialism and
cruelty?
Whose countries are African countries in reality?

When humans behave like simians
Such humans dehumanise themselves
Simians have short memories
Humans, especially a nation should never act like simians
Sometimes, simians are better because they laugh at each
other
Yet, they don't hate or kill each other

You may hate one another
You may kill each other
You may call name to each other
Yet, Africa as your mother
Has never stopped loving you
Africa has never stopped crying for your disunity
Africa will never stop screaming about witnessing your
brutality
Who bewitched you brutes?

As mortals, you may look at the soil and laugh at it

You too my ignore and abuse it
It has never stopped singing the songs of life and freedom
Learn this from me
The land speaks quite loudly though you are unable to
hear it
Its songs nourish you and everything
Have you ever thought about this hidden Truth?

Berlin-cloned Nations

Dear African Brothers and Sisters
Do you still remember the history of the Berlin
Conference?
It is the colonial conference that partitioned and divided
Africa
It happened in 1884 when Europe connived to colonise
Africa
When Africans discriminate against Africans based on
their nationality
They blindly commit colonial criminality
Why are you doing its ominous job of perpetually keeping
Africa divided and exploited?
Before the disastrous Berlin Conference
Africa was loosely one by nature as a single geographical
and political entity
Strong and independent, Africa was among the
community of the world
Its needs and used to fully and perpetually cater
Then, the fatal Berlin conference created a perpetual
aperture
The fracture on which many Africans failed to put a
closure
As the ace Chinua Achebe would narrate
There came Things Fall Apart
The bond that kept us together was cut
The people who organically were united were set apart
It is at this notorious meeting everything was cut asunder
It was nothing but the conference that committed our
murder
Knowing the danger such sabotage posed
Some African founders put the hope on the future
With the belief that Africans would reunite Africa
Where is African now?

Unification of Africa did never happen up until now
Instead, Africa is fracturing more and more
Ethiopia that used to be one is no more
It produced Ethiopia and Eretria
Sudan that used to be one is long gone
It was divide between two Sudan and South Sudan
Somalia that used to be one is long dead, in tiny clan states
is now divided
When will this happen amidst such self-hate like the ones
in South Africa?
How will this happen while every African country defines
itself as a nation?
Who will unite Africa?

Remember Ghana's Kwame Nkrumah
What of Congo's Patrice Lumumba?
Don't forget Tanzania's Mwalimu Julius K. Nyerere
Remember Guinea's Ahmed Sekou Touré
Never forget Ethiopia's Haile Selassie
Instrumental was Zambia's Kenneth Kaunda
These were the champions of Africa reunification
However, as the time faded
Africa has never seen any union
Some tried and failed
Remember the Senegambia?
It was myopically failed
Even the federal Ethiopia suffered the same
Successful and ever-standing is Tanzania
Its United republic of Tanzania has survived the test of
time
Somalia soon will become history
Just as was the case for Sudan

Nobody talks about hands-on unification of Africa
anymore
There is this so-called African union

Has it ever attempted to reunite Africa?
It is but only a good moniker
Practically, the thing is dividing Africa

Dear Africans and All Oppressed Ones
Our contemporary rulers have miserably failed us
We too, as citizenry, have helplessly failed ourselves
We both have collectively failed Africa and its future
Do we need donors to unite Africa?
Aren't we the agents of colonisation by proxy?
Anybody who denies this should come forth
Let him or her come, I will show them the illogicality
Aren't Africans carrying colonial identities they call
nationality
Who created those entities?

Dear Africans, Brothers and Sisters
We are blindly and shamelessly proud of being South
Africans
Franticly, proud of being Tanzanians
Cameroonians and Ambazonians
As we naïvely do this, our masters are laughing at us
They wonder who bewitched us
We, who can pointlessly celebrate our perpetual demise
There are crucial questions we need to us ourselves
As well, we need to be honest to ourselves
Who created these entities and named them for us?
Is it their *cogito ergo sum* that excluded us?
Why and how'd we keep subscribing to twisted ideologies?
We need to stop devouring such colonial mythologies
We need to do this without any apologies
We all know who sold us
We know, as well, who buy us
We even know who eat us
Partially or with gung-ho onus
Doesn't history say so?

What have we learned from history?
Repeating the same errors!
Internalising and maintaining colonial dregs
Tell me please

Dear African Brothers and Sisters
The one who created these fake and toxic entities
destroyed Africa
Cameroonians are butchering each other along the lines of
their colonial masters
Those that used to be Africans before becoming
Cameroonians
Are now Cameroonians and Ambazonians
Whatever they are doesn't help them but antagonise them
One people of the same family treat each other as
foreigners!
Aren't these the people of the same totem?
Who bewitched Africa?
Oh, poor Africa
Mother Africa

Dear Black Africans
Yes, black ones; for there are those who don't want to be
Africans
They still though are Africans
I don't intend to discriminate against them
Though they discriminate against me
Go to the countries in the so-called Maghreb
Aren't Africans denying being African but Arab?
Ask them who they are called when they go to real Arabs
They are called Africans
Like Boers called Africans kaffirs
Some Africans, in the name of religion, still refer to each
other as kaffirs!
Others call other people slaves

Dear African Brothers and Sisters
Let's stop behaving like simians
Do you know what simians do to others?
They just laugh at each other's buttocks
They attack farms as they laugh
As if they once held mattocks

I reprimand South Africans
I do so the same way I do Rwandans who killed each
other because of this madness
Cameroonians are now butchering each other fighting of
fake nationalisms
In the CAR Africans are killing each other for their
religious differentials
Nigerians are killing each other under the madness of
foreign isms
Currently, your Mozambican neighbours are suffering the
same illness!
Look at the Central African Republic
Everything is ethnically frantic and pedantic
Africans are brazenly and idiotically killing each other
Aren't Christians and Muslims butchering each other?
Ask them why
They will tell you they are of different religions!
Because of this Afrophobia, terrorist groups are cashing
Like never before they are recruiting
The arms industry is making a killing
Illicit weapons are smuggled in such fake nations to be
used to kill ignorant and innocent people
Thanks to this Afrophobia, many innocent people have
been killed
Property worth billions and zillions have been destroyed
Poverty is increasing while animosity is getting a bed

Thanks to xenophobia and Afrophobia
Religions are exporting their toxic ideologies to Africa

Africans are picking them up blindly
Where today do you see Arabs butchering each other
because of ideology
Where do you see Europeans discriminating against
Europeans because of ideology?
Arabs are Arabs first and next something
Practically, exactly, in the same way
Europeans are whites then something
For them, everything white is something exceptional
So, too, everything black is diabolical

What difference does it have from what is ensuing in
South Africa?
South Africa is not lonely
Go to Somalia where a brother is killing another
Don't forget Libya where Africans are selling Africans
Visit Mali and Mauritania where Africans are enslaving
each other
Ask them what went wrong and why
They will hide under colour differentiations
They are all black, but others think others are blacker than
them
Ask them who they are, they will scamper under fake
identities and mere bunkum
Some will tell you, just like South Africans, that they are
Muslims
Others will say they are Christians
Aren't they Africans first and the rest last?

What difference does it have if the end product is
Afrophobia?
Afrophobes are like any other xenophobes regardless their
utopia
Whatever sets Africans against each other is lethal and
mere mania

A black Boer has no difference from a white racial
megalomania
Apartheid perpetrated by Africans is as worse as the one
white enacted

We tend to blame white colonial monsters
This doesn't mean that we should not
Nevertheless, we go to bed with black colonial monsters
Aren't those ignoring Afrophobia homemade colonisers?
Aren't those clinging to Berlin-demarcated borders
colonisers
To me, the latter is worse than the former
The former was not related to us
While the latter is related to us

Dear South Africans
In this you are not unaccompanied
Like any other Africans who go around in pride
Those who pride themselves that they are free in Berlin-
sired borders
How can they be truly free while they're divided and
became feeble?
A disunited Africa will always not only be a laughable fable
It also will remain a scandalous and fickle
Isn't Africa colonised by its own people?
Do you know those who colonise Africa?
Let me jog your mind a wee bit
You call them presidents and the high and the mighty
They make you believe they are your liberators
Aren't they the same collaborators?
I mean those who fight for their pots
Yet, they tell you they are for you
If they aren't, why then have they failed to unite Africa
miserably?
Look at this and think reasonably
How will they liberate you from themselves?

Do you know they're the ones who hang a big stone on
your collars?
In dollars, dinars, francs, yens and renminbi among others

Like constipated houseflies, they puke everywhere
They are always in their fantasy and childlike idiosyncrasy
They bulldoze and brutalize you; and call it democracy
Though, they are manning a modern people
They still live in their hidden hypocrisy
While your lives end up in crises
They think those they rule are their tools
Yes, the tools they can use as they deem fit
Just think about this a bit
To them, their subjects are illiterates if not boobs
That is why our elites have always sat on our shoulders
They make us dance and sing according to their songs
With their tummies full of sins, they are everywhere
They make you believe they represent you while they
actually represent their tummies
You die in miseries while they live in extravagancies
When they have eaten you have
When they are safe you are
Are you really?

Dear Africans of every comportment
How can Africa be independent under milliards of
presidents?
Who needs them now while we know they are the
creatures of coloniality?
Who needs them while they have always served their
colonial masters?
Aren't Africans colonised by such African presidents
I like to call them homegrown colonisers
Yes, they preside over internalised internal colonisation

Dear Brothers and Sisters

I am taking our rulers on not out of hatred
It is not out of fantasy or *holier than thou*
These are but criminals who vend you
It is out of what they have always delivered
Haven't they delivered themselves on our expenses?
Look at their posh lives compared to our glum ones
Who is enjoying the freedom fir which we all fought
dearly?

We need to interrogate and shame our rulers
We need to ask them tough questions
What's their *post-facto* response to Africa's woes?
Aren't they the *de facto* root causes of our woes?
Aren't they really sucking-political beasts?
Yes, those that for over five decades are keeping Africa
undone
Aren't they the obstacles towards the unification of
Africa?
Who is stopping them from reunifying Africa?
Who is stopping them from vending Africa?
Aren't our rulers vending us like fish and carrots?

Can such colonisers and those making do with them laugh
at South Africa?
Many have clung to their statehouses
For them, independence is about their presidency
Their personal power is what they call independence
Africa's independence is a chicanery
What has it ever brought to the citizenry apart from
miseries?
Are South Africans and other Africans really free?
Are those being persecuted by them truly free
Is Africa truly free?
If it is, when and how
I would like to know
If we are all free

Who is free and who is not?

Priding ourselves that we are independent is a big affront
How can we be independent while our countries are
dependent?
How can we be independent while we discriminate against
others?
How can we be independent while we hate others?
Think about this my brethren
Dig deeper into your hearts
Has Africa ever been independent?
Hopefully, this makes sense for dum-dums

Our rulers preach colonialism in the name of
independence
Why'd Africans carry passports with them to travel in their
Africa?
Why'd Africans bear many nationalities as if Africa wasn't
a single nation?
Why are Africans poorer than all while they sit on
humungous resources?
Why are Africans discriminated against almost by every
race?
Yes, they are discriminated against by everybody
Go to Europe and see how they are dying in the
Mediterranean
Go to the US and see how they are called shitholes and all
nonsense
Go to Asia and see how they are called *kalu, absii* or apes
Go to South Africa and evidence how they are
discriminated against
Go see how they are robbed by their kin
See how they are necklaced by their brethren
See how they are killed like vermin

Whoever preaches colonial sovereignty must be a colonial
agent
If anything, this is what South Africa seems to perfect
Though South Africa is not alone in this apathy
Why is Africa still divided after many decades?
All African states still regard themselves as republics while
they actually are not
Show me an independent African state by the meaning of
the word

When South Africa gained its independence
The whole Africa was elated
for its shock nonetheless
Slowly, the leopard started showing its true spots
What many wrongly thought was gold
Indeed, it wasn't but mere gangue
South Africans started to play *holier than thou*
Methodically, this has gone on though
Where is the government?

To know how this criminality has been replicated
Year after year, it has surfaced
South Africans think are better than the rest
They too are different from the rest
Take or leave it
This is the fact
Had they been the same, they would desist committing
criminality
Now, that they have become oppressors
Yes, the oppressed have become oppressors
The preys have become the predators
What will I call them for the matter of fact?

Had South Africans been Africans just like others
Would they discriminate against others?
Had South Africans been African though they are

Would they kill and rob others who happen to be their
colleagues?
Even goats and other beasts know their colleagues
This doesn't need any religion to preach
It doesn't need any teacher to teach
This is an inborn knowledge every beast needs to possess
However, for South Africans and other racists, the truth is
totally unalike
Practically, *holier than thou* affinity is their instinct
If you are not like me, you are not praiseworthy

Those who hate their African origin will always be
Africans
They must know they are but Africans
Even if they dupe themselves that they are not Africans
The world will show them who they truly are, Africans
How could Africans discriminate against Africans?
Non-Africans are wondering and laughing at Africans
Many Africans are discriminated against wherever they go
Go to Europe currently and see what they encounter
Those that they once accommodated have turned against
them
Those who came and colonised them are now evading
them
Even those that were shipped to the Americas do the
same
Who invaded another first?
Who brought the miseries and inequality?
Aren't those who colonised laughing at Africans that are
now killing one another?
Why can't you see such simple historical fact!

Philosopher Paulo Freire was dead right
When any oppressed bays to become an oppressor
Know that there is a very big difficulty
Who else on earth, for long, suffered from apartheid?

The answer is clearly simple that it is today's oppressor
The one found in South Africa is the one
Why people don't learn from history
History would avert them replicating the same sin they
once suffered
South Africa, please revisit your history

Who would fathom it that this would happen?
Who would stomach such an *en masse* forgetful sin?
It has taken me some years to believe this could happen
I still am saddened that Mandela's country would end in
this ignominy
It haunts me so to speak when truth stares at me
Aren't the Africans the South Africans are killing today
that liberated it?
Aren't the same that sacrificed everything to see to it that
Africa is free?
Wow, they had such a wrong midframe
That charity begins at home
Then was then, not now South Africa's replicated shame

Where is collective awareness and understanding?
Please someone tell me; I am pleading
Is the root cause of South African miseries the other
Africans?
Where do we put systemic corruption in this ragbag?
Call this, if you may, South African mbaqanga
Where do we put endemic economic discrimination?
Abomination, abomination, abomination!
Whom do we hold accountable?
This is the question everybody needs to answer
We need a clear answer
Yes, a clear answer not a fable

Why Acting Like Simians?

Dear Africans
There is an African tale of thoughtless simians
Remember simians?
I hope all of you know these quarrelsome creatures
What crazy organisms!
Destruction is one of their cultures
Simians are funny beasts to watch when naughty
All simians share one important nexus
They are forgetful and myopic; yet they think they are nifty
They are just like other beasts though they actually are
toplofty
This is the story of two simians
One day two simians were doing their monkey business
One started laughing as it stared at another simian
All simians in the troupe started to query

Consider and look at what the simian in question did
As simians were congregating on a hill
This gullible simian saw the back of the other mandrill
It started laughing at another simian
All simians were shocked
Others openly abhorred
They asked the sniggering simian what it was laughing at
Thoughtlessly and shamelessly, the simian responded
It pointed at the rumps of another
"Don't you see its bottom", it confidently said
All simians were annoyed and punished the one of theirs

We may ignorantly laugh at simians
On laughing at each other we may
But this never have you to sway
Look at the simians the other away
When it comes to unity

Simians are ahead of us
A group of simian fights together
They become ominous even to bigger animals like a
leopard
They always sleep together
They hunt together and live together
The better part of simians is that they just laughed at each
other
This is different from Africans killing one another

Are we becoming the inane simian that laughed at
another?
Did it know that every simian predicament is but similar?
Annoyed and dismayed is me upon this to ponder
How can humans behave like simians and be safer?
Aren't simians the beasts which know not their future?
When humans behave the same way, it becomes a disaster
That is why sadly and without any remorse, I utter
It is hard to maintain and encounter though is the fact of
the matter
For wrong reasons South Africa has become another
disaster

Apartheid reduced South Africans to a laughingstock
Its people, like horses, are still manned with a hidden
sjambok
Africa stood firm to see to it that this came to a stop
It still is with total anguish, dismay and shock
That the same South Africa would replicate this peccadillo
It abhors beyond any human even animal imaginable flair
When a prey of yesterday become a predator of today
Is it because of small memory or lack of it?
Is it the rationale that the spear is good for a pig?
How could the victims of yesterday forget their dilemma?
How could they easily and quickly replicate the same?

Isn't South Africa enacting the same crime it suffered
yesterday?

Afrophobic South Africa is Africa's cancer
No African can escape its curse
All Africans are into it either willingly or not
Therefore, we need to take a note
Afrophobia, like xenophobia, is a deadly ailment
What a perilous illness!
It is a type of mental disease that curtails the power to
think
Ignorance and fake importance are its products
It becomes even deadly when sufferers discriminate
against
Those of their own like has been the case in South Africa
Xenophobia and Afrophobia by Africans against Africans!
Unbelievable as it may sound, though there's no good
xenophobia
It becomes worse when it becomes intra-phobia

Like any quickly spreading contagion
In South Africa, Afrophobia enjoys affection
It is alive and well amidst the nation
That is why authorities have never put a stop to it
It is the same as was that of yesterday
Cancer will always be cancer; and this is very clear
Africa needs to unite against this malignance
Africa needs to ask for right answers shall it aim at
successes
Africa needs to draw a line in the sand
To see to it that South Africa is made accountable
It strongly and urgently needs to shun South Africa
without any clemency
Had this been predated, South Africa would still be
grappling with apartheid

Who would pay by his or her economy and blood for the
country that will kill its citizenry?
If any, this must be naïve and silly

Looking at the history of xenophobic attacks shamelessly
replicated in South Africa
One conclusion comes to my mind *vis-à-vis* South Africa
and the rest of Africa
How'd xenophobia define Africa and still it remains the
same?
Don't we hear of slavery in the Maghreb that denies being
African?
To me, this sin is alive and well and yet the same
Despite what, Africa will always be one and the same
Apartheid, xenophobic and Afrophobic attacks and
slavery are the same
They share the same bond that, for Africa, they are but
embarrassment
Yes, it is nothing or anything near but shame
I have tried as hard as I could to find a name
What I know is shame, shame, shame *ad infinitum*

Ignorant as anybody can be in this matter
When Afrophobic attacks happened
I tried as hard I could to define the phenomenon
I tried to look at the colour of the perpetrator
I examined the colour of the sufferer
I admit that all the same
They share almost everything save their ignorance
The difference is that racists are venomous
Out of racists victims need to squeeze the malice

Ironically, when it comes to who they truly are
They are deadly creatures everybody needs to abhor
They yodel about discrimination by Boers
Aren't Boers South Africans like other Africans?

Blacks are accusing Boers of monopolising their economy
And indeed, the Boers control South African economy
This is true though claimed by wrong people who replicate
the same
If South Africans need justice, they must do justice

Although we tend to blame rogue South Africans
The picture is bigger than this one can imagine
Where do we put politicians who provoke such attacks?
Why are we busy with blaming the small fish as we ignore
the sharks?
Where do we put the government that sleeps at the
trundle?
Where do we put those who enacted apartheid and
maintained it economically?
All such things need to be considered shall we aspire to
solve the problem

South Africa is stinky with mindboggling inequality
The *hoi polloi* needs to take on the *hoity toity* who benefit
from this inequity
Those who corrupted and sold South Africa
Those who pretend to represent the paupers that they end
up vending
Those who represent their stomachs under the umbrella of
democracy
This is what the trodden ones need to ponder on earnestly

Nobody should monopolise the economy except the
people
Nobody should monopolise land except the people
Even power must belong to the people
Are the people aware of this while are targeting a wrong
foe?

Racism is racism regardless what
Racism is racism even if committed by a simian
Racism is evil even if it is played by a ruffian
The colour of the racist is immaterial
The aim of the racist is pointless as well
A racist is a racist regardless he or she is a compatriot
A black racist is as evil as the white racist is
Racism is the tool of inhumanity
Humans should never be racists
How, if at all, they are weaker than beasts?
I have never seen a sheep discriminating against a cow
Surely, in this very milieu
Never have I seen an opossum discriminate a kangaroo
Have you ever seen a pigeon discriminate against dove?

Racism is the worst thing a sane person can embark on
Racism, just like any form of criminality, is an abomination
Those who discriminate against others are no different
from demons
They may say they're guarding their nation or whatever
notion
If anything, indeed, racism is a tool of chicken-hearted
morons
It becomes even worse when the whole nation subscribes
to discrimination
I don't know what to say or call such a disgraceful nation
Phew! It downs on me, especially when the racist nation is
African
As it commits this crime against those of its own

Africa has always been discriminated against almost by
everybody
Considering what happened in South Africa
Mandela must be turning in his grave
This is not the country he was imprisoned for
It can't be the country he was ready to shed his blood for

Never, never, this cannot be Africa
Sisulu must be grieving with rage
Solomon Mahlangu must be crying never-endingly
Steve Biko must be sick as he raves
What can South Africa tell such heroes?

I feel sickened when I remember the icons of deliverance
Where will Desmond Tutu put his face?
Where will De Klerk put his face?
It must be hard for such icons to stomach
How can they make do with collective shame?
It is sacrilegious for them to be part of
They fought for freedom not racism
They fought for realism but not nihilism

Dear South Africans
Just like for entire Africa, the fight for freedom is not over
yet
Freedom needs to be seen on your tables
Freedom needs to be felt in your tummies
Freedom needs to be seen in your schools
Freedom is not about the flag that many flaunt
When you go there for education it must be felt in your
heads
Freedom needs to be felt in your streets, safe streets
Freedom needs to be enjoyed in your residences
Freedom is the land but not a piece of cloth many like to
boast about
Freedom is apolitical
Freedom is practical

Dear African Brothers and Sisters
I know how you all aspire to be truly free
You truly need true freedom
Freedom that will redeem your grabbed land
Freedom that will redress your exploited blood

Freedom that will tell the truth about the world
Yes, freedom that history one day will tell
That there was a world of racism as the means of
prosperity for racists
Those who used colour as the pretexts of slavery and
colonialism
Those whose prosperity was made by exploiting Africa
Those who sold and bought Africans
Those who still exploit Africa and whatever isms

To *ubaba* Desmond Tutu, specifically I am writing
I know how you feel and the way you have always
responded
One of the things that propelled me to write this epistle is
your response
You wrote the president when chaos occurred
You didn't cower or hide behind any ruse
Thanks for your unwavering commitment to justice

I wish *ubaba* Mandela were around
He would not stand aside and look
How could he while this betrays his vision?
I believe whatever it would take
You two would not let this happen again
Again, Mandela is long gone
Alone as you stand
Ubaba Tutu, please keep the embers on
Shall the rulers ignore you for their liability
You just fulfil your responsibility

What Is the Issue?

South Africans badly need to get to the bottom of their problems
Collectively, they need to know their real problems
This will save them from the canard of racism
Facing reality will avert them their killing venom becoming collective killers
Are those they are now killing the problem?
Will their deaths and expulsion solve the problem?
Let us think like a society of humans not simians
What is the issue?

Some think the so-called foreigners are taking their jobs
Where are these jobs?
A casual work wants to be paid like a doctor
Where will these jobs come from without accommodating the reality?
South Africans don't want menial jobs
Many of them think such jobs are for peasantry
This is when every non-South African is painted with the same thicket
Even those unskilled want high wage!
If there is the war that you need to wage
It is nothing but taking up any available jobs
Are South Africans ready to do such jobs?
They assert the foreigners take low payments
This makes South Africans lose opportunities for employment
Really?
Whom to blame in such mistreatments if South African despise such jobs?
Where are the employments amidst stinking inequalities?
Who employs whom and who works for whom to get what?

Can a largely unequal society provide that what people want?
Isn't this a thorny issue South Africans need to address and arrest first?
Will Afrophobia create jobs while the oppressor is still the same?
Will the killings of innocent and poor Africans shake the oppressor?
What do you call this when the oppressed become oppressors?

I know black and poor South Africans face penury
This is the fate of many Africans almost in every country
Again, are Afrophobic attacks the key?
Who stands in their way
Are the so-called foreigners or their rulers?
Who is their true enemy between foreigners and rulers?
Does this need a PhD in political science or economics to see?

Afrophobia seems to metamorphose
Consider what will happen shall its victims replicate it
Nigerians and Zambians have already warned
Who will triumph without peace?
You kill some in your country
They torch your businesses in their country
This way madness takes a new deadly turn
Fire by fire and an eye for an eye becomes justice
What an injustice for victims to become perpetrators!
Two wrongs don't make a right

In conjunction with other, Africans liberated their country from apartheid
This is an indisputable and unsubtle fact
It will always remain like that

Has their so-called independence brought what they
expected?
Have the promises that were made been fulfilled?
Why were they not met in the first place?
When will these promises be fulfilled?
Who owns what between South Africans and their rulers?
Who is vending who between South Africans and their
rulers?
These are crucial questions every reasonable South African
needs to ask
Will the killing of the so-called foreigners resolve the
problems?
These are the questions our rulers must provide answers
to

Often times, the media is awash with vile pictures
The pictures of the killings and tortures
With dismay, the world is laughing at every African
Africa is wondering what went wrong in South Africa
Africans are portrayed as beasts because of this
viciousness
Even those who sold them in slavery are now hooting
Those who bought and used them are laughing
Those who enacted colonialism are smiling
As they prepare themselves to come and broker peace
Really!
Do we really need their *service*?
Has South Africa become such useless!
What went wrong?
Will South Africa keep on going to the dogs?

Dear Brothers and sisters,
We need to carefully and seriously search our depths
Courageously, we need to question our conscience
Let us put aside our myopic and narrow grievances
Does Africa really deserve this in the first place?

Do Africans deserve this disservice?
What went wrong?

I know; the majority of black South Africans are landless
What used to be hope has become bleakness
They're promised land by their freedom fighters
Almost thirty years down the line they have nothing to
actualise!
They promised reconciliation but the promise has long
evaporated
So, too, long gone is the hope that Mandela preached
Whom do you blame this on?
I know the so-called foreigners are similarly landless
They have nothing but bob-a-job to live on
What of those sitting on millions of acres of land?
What of the land that is not worked on?
How much land is sitting idle?
What is the issue?
Isn't this the issue?

South African Economy

Everybody knows the real situation for fact
For yet another time and reason, let me clearly restate it
It seems South Africans have pointlessly maintained
insipidity
The economy benefits the minority
While the majority has been upset
Instead of addressing the very problem, why are you
employing brutality?
Instead of taking the real problem on, why are you
creating another problem pointlessly?
Don't South Africans know the exploitative nature of their
economy?
Don't and can't they see this economic apartheid!
Are they such blind?
Have they indifferently forgotten their true history?
Don't they know who owns what and who doesn't?
Does this need donor to come and elaborate?

No doubt in my mind
South African economy is but an anomaly
It is the only economy that hinges on the colour
It is a totally colonised economy
It has no different from those of the US and Canada
It resembles that of Australia
All those economies above are built on racism
Their foundations are built on stinking apartheid
It is time now to decolonise such economies
These are but the economies of the bullies
Such economies need to equally and profitably serve
everybody
Abandon apartheid economy as you embark on national
economy

Go ask your true economists; they'll tell you
Professionally, they are, indeed, amenable
When it comes to your quandaries, just like you do, they
know who is responsible
This is the very painful truth that many do not want to
face
Stop shifting culpability to innocent black brothers and
sisters
Cum grano salis go quiz your politicians who hoodwink you
Yes, the ones that vend you
Aren't they the beneficiaries of the inequity they've
boomed on?
If needs be, go ask even the Guptas aka Zuptas
There's no economy on earth with discrepancy like South
African
This is the problem number one
No economy in Africa is racialized like South African one
By all account, this can be the first hunch of the problem
Think about it, you will see what you have never seen
Ponder on its consequences, you will unearth the missing
connection

Dear South African brothers and sisters
Please, do carefully revisit your history without any kernel
of prejudice or nescience
Do so without any intentional blindness
Your true history will give you the tool of addressing your
true glitches
Go back to the time when your land was grabbed
You know who grabbed it
This is the time when colour became the capital of
acquiring land and riches
Do you call those who grabbed your land names?
You can't
Because they're South Africans like anybody after you
pardoned them

Who owns your minerals?
Who owns and runs your banks?
Who corrupts your governments?
I know all those are not *amakwerekwere*
How much have *amakwerekwere* ever owned?
I know these questions are provocative
Importantly, they have a special purpose to serve
These are the questions mentally mature people need to ask
These are the very questions that must be given right answers
Whom will you ask these questions?
As a nation, you need a serious dialogue

Who practically owns South Africa in practical terms?
Are you who vote or those who own the land
Who? Tell me, please
Are the politicians and their courtiers or the *hoi polloi*?
Tell me the true owners of South Africa that you pride yourselves about
These are the questions South Africans need to seriously ask and answer
Killing the so-called foreigners will never generate any answer
Instead, it is exacerbating the problem
It is wise to stop such collective blindness and self-destruction

Go further without any gist of mindlessly fear
Who grabbed your land and used for hundreds of years whereupon you suffer?
Who's worse between land grabbers and these illusory foreigners?
How come Africans are becoming foreigners in their continent but not the others?

Isn't this intra-racism blindly perpetrated by the Africans against Africans?

Do not replicate apartheid
Doing so is not only travesty but also evil
Apartheid was built on fear and vitriol
Practically, Afrophobia is another apartheid
The difference is that it is committed by blacks against blacks
Apartheid is apartheid whether committed by whites or blacks
No venom is good despite what
No hatred is constructive despite who is behind it
No poison is needed otherwise applied to vermin
Poison is the same even if made from a tree or animal

Dear South Africans
Do you know the precedent you are setting for your own peril?
Look at how silent the world is pretending that this is an African problem
Loathe or love me if you wish
Such response is nothing but gibberish
You are growing an appetite that'll lead you to attacking non-Africans
the day you'll do this you'll see how the world will stand quickly and firmly
Don't you know you are making your own future as Africans eviler

Is Africa Becoming A Laughingstock

When I ponder on what is ongoing in South Africa
I wonder what Africa is becoming
Is Africa becoming a laughingstock?
Are landlessness South Africans going to retain their land?
Our friends are crying when they look at how we are
screwing up
Is this the way South Africans are organised to address
their bottleneck?
Africa is howling in anguish, dismay and shame
Tears of blood are gushing as innocent people die
Others are wondering as others yelp without any help
How could the authorities condone such a thing!
Against all odds, how could Africans enact such a thing!
Why the victim of yesterday is becoming the perpetrator
of today?
I seriously would like to know why
It is painful and damning to evidence it
Afrophobia is haunting and truly tormenting
Afrophobia is saddening and abhorring
How could we easily and quickly turn ourselves into
orgies?
Afrophobia is gory just like any other goriness
It is lugubrious
We need to fight it at all costs
We need to fight it to avoid Africa from becoming a
laughingstock

How can a Brother discriminate against a Brother?
How can a brother hate another?
I call upon sages and philosophers
please come and help us out here
How can a sister laugh when someone tortures or kills her
sister?

I see daughters of Africa in South Africa as they holler
Celebrating the tortures of their sisters
Some are singing
While others are cheering
How can this happen in Africa!
Shock
Shock
Shock without end
Ambuye, please save Africa from self-inflicted wounds

How come they've easily forgotten?
That we're one nation of Africa
How come they did not learn?
They refused to learn just from their plight of yesterday
We saw them and heard their cry
It was at the time Boers discriminated against Africans
How come they're enacting the same?
As if they are halfwits and hoodlums
They call their crime love of nationalism
This is but escapism
It is purely scapegoatism
If we face it in its true system
Is Afrophobia really nationalism?
Are killings of innocent people patriotism?
No, this is but sheer hooliganism
It is nothing but vampirism
Yes, it is indeed mental botulism

Many criminals take camouflage in nationalism
Shame on all of them who abuse the concept of
nationalism
All those criminals enacting racism based on their bent
rationalism
This is but bunkum under whatever prism
How can nationalism thrive by the way of racism?

Such misguided and racist nationalism is nothing but pure
hoodlumism
It is nothing but sheer neo-Nazism wrapped in fake
nationalism
Weren't those enacting this racism yesterday's victims?
How can one differentiate them from their persecutors?
How if at all they all depend on colonial borders?

Those replicating racism openly seem not to know their
true antiquity
Borders are but a superimposition we need to fight and
deracinate
Borders were created to divide and weaken Africans
Yes, look at how they are tearing each other guarding such
colonial devices
Please, my brethren South Africans
Stop Afrophobia
It won't help us as Africans
It won't help us as humans

Why are you becoming oppressors?
You were yesterday the oppressed ones
Have you easily forgotten?
What a loss!
What went wrong within such a short period of
emancipation?
Do you reminisce?
Many African countries supported your cause
At the time you were fighting against apartheid
Is this how you can pay their generosity by killing other
Africans
Folks,
Stop Afrophobia
It won't help us

Many African countries ruined their economies

They sacrificed everything to see to it that South Africa
becomes free
Now that the same we fought for are in a freak killing
spree
Turning tables on those who enhanced them to be free
Isn't this sheer madness and ignominy?
Isn't this sheer insanity
Committed under the name of nationality
Now that you have forgotten
You've turned yourselves into beasts
You have abused our generosity
You've misused our charity
You've chosen Afrophobia
You molested our filia
Please stop Afriphobia
Africa is one
Mungu, reunite us

What a precedent you are now setting?
By discriminating against, butchering and hating your own
brethren
Do you know folks?
You have enacted a new form of racism
Stinking one even more than apartheid
Racism of black against another!
Phew
Please brethren
Think again,
Think twofold
Afrophobia won't do us good
Mungu protect us from this malady

Decolonise Your Country

Dear Brother and Sisters
I have this to urge you as another solution to the problem
Think about your freedom
Interrogate it and see if it serves you as any *binadam*
To solve the problem, please decolonise your country
Get it rid of colonial names and legacies
Instead of attacking your brothers and sisters
Why don't cleanse South Africa off apartheid relics
Don't you know you are one of messed economies on earth?
Don't you know that you are among countries that lost their identity?
Look at your cities with all such stinking colonial names
Let me remind you of these dirty names
I always hear Johannesburg and Pietermaritzburg
Who are these Johannes and Pieter to your country?
Where is Mandelasburg and Tutumaritzburg?
I see Pretoria where there is no Shaka Zulu city?
I hear people talk about port Elizabeth
Where is port Madikzela?
You have mountain Drakensberg
Why have failed to restore its actual name Ukhahlamba?
Why don't you call Durban Sobukwetown?
Whose county is your country?
Who is eating your country while you are complaining?
Who is enjoying while what you know is nothing but pains?

Let us face the reality
We need to openly tell South Africans
That they are becoming neo-colonialists
They have to differentiate from apartheid architects
And this is the fact

Africans from neighbouring states are not a liability
They just work hard just like anybody else
They toil and suffer just like any South African pauper
The problem lies somewhere else
Methinks it is uneven division of resources
That has created all this mess
So, please address this mess
Instead of killing innocent persons

I know some immigrants indulge themselves in criminal
activities
Just like any other South Africans
This is human nature
Whenever such a thing happens, a person must be judged
according to actions
Crimes are not accepted anywhere in any society
Those indulging in criminal activities should be brought to
book
Whoever that does illegal things must know he or she is
on the hook

Go ask fat cats in the upper echelons of power
Those who eat the country and its earthlings
Ask the elites who share the same table with the fat
moggies
Aren't they that enjoy Africa's beauties?
Don't they feel and represent their own tummies?
Yet, they go around cheating the masses
Why are they eating alone while the majority is suffering?
Why while the mass is in abject manmade poverty
This is the contentious bone many bigwigs like to avert
Afrophobia is a pretext many failed politicians seem to
invest in
Either resulting from political bankruptcy if not
unreasonableness
Such skinny politicos do cash on bigotry and ineptness

For the nation to forge ahead, it must avoid these vices
There's no answer in such a stance
There's no future in such collective recklessness

Dear Sisters and Brothers
Africa is now laughed at even by those it is supposed to
laugh at
Thanks to what you enacted, many are upset and can't get
it
Again, I don't blame everybody
For what's been going on in South Africa
Where people from neighbouring are robbed
They are tortured
They are killed
They are told to pack and evaporate
This is unfair my brothers and sisters
Stop this curse
Africa is for all Africans
Mungu, restore our oneness

Go to Mandela's grave and repent
Visit Solomon Mahlangu's tomb and regret
Go there and tear your garments
Tell them to forgive and forget
You've turned yourselves into serpents
Now, you're killing your relatives
Tomorrow, you will kill your children and wives
Once killers always killers
Please avoid this curse
The curse of Afrophobia
Mungu hear our prayers

Do you remember Shaka Zulu's impis
They were real soldiers not imps
They fought for dignity, freedom and peace
They loathed carnage, colonialism and violence

Now that you are pointlessly in chaos
Please go back to the books
Maybe, you will see the light
Modimo show us the light so that we can do right things
Show us the way so that we can pursue right strategies

Do you remember Mandela's guiding philosophy?
His was real love without any atrophy
Mandela took a clear way
The way to autonomy
Don't turn his vision into infamy
Solve problems peacefully
Do everything carefully
Know that you are making a gory history
Unkulukulu, restore our glory

I am told you only targeted neighbouring Africans
Only Africans!
You spared others from even afar
Isn't this new type of racism?
That involves people of the same race
I call this intra-racism
It is more dangerous than the one that white racists
invented
Stop it; it is horrid
Today you are killing Africans
Whom will you take on after they are all gone?
The answer is obvious
You will turn to whites and Indians and others
Once you are done with those
Then, you'll turn against each other
This is when you'll need a refuge
Where will you go?
Thixo, grant us your refuge

Is there any need of going this destructive and diabolic
way really?
Is discrimination or Afrophobia the solution to your
problems really?
Try to think twice
You may be able to address the real problem
Instead of creating fake one that will mislead you even
further
Try to think in terms of history
Where were you yesterday?
You were but mere victims of apartheid
Why are you now victimizing others who helped you to
slay apartheid?
Apartheid is a crime
Yes, the crime against humanity
It only brings resentment
It is the source of national embarrassment
Let's condemn and fight it
Whoever that commits it
He or she who commits an offense
Be he or she African
Be he black or white
He or she is but a stinking racist
Racists are criminals
Criminals deserve to rot behind bars
Nwali show us the light

How Can You Easily Forget?

Dear Brothers and Sisters from South Africa
Have you easily forgotten your true history?
What went wrong?
Please tell me so that I can help all along
I still believe in true African brotherhood
I miss practical African sisterhood
I still aspire for African unity and oneness
For, Africa is supposed to be regarding itself as one blood
We need to have African one purpose
Based on our true and practical unity and oneness
Stop Afrophobia; it isn't the answer
Mwari hear our prayer

Afrophobia is a crime and a mania
If anything, it is nothing but mega megalomania
It is a product of high-pitched myopia
It naturally causes mega mania
This should not be your way
Xikwembu show us the straight way

Afrophobia is naturally counterproduction
It amounts to self-destruction as a nation
Please, seriously take my recantation
Afrophobia is a sin
It should not be the take of any nation
Please, stop Afrophobia
Instead, look at what the problem is
Then, find the way to resolve it
Killing innocent people is of no service
It, indeed, will ruin you as a nation
Please brothers and sisters in South Africa
Stop Afrophobic attacks
Zumbe hear our prayers

Dear Brothers and Sisters
Critically, study your history
You'll avoid this self-inflicted political purgatory
True history is never perfunctory
Study the noble history of Africa as well
Now that you know as indicated prior
Those boundaries and nationalities you are proud of
Are nothing but the creatures of colonial masters to take
you for a ride
Have you allowed yourselves to keep on being taken for a
ride?
Wow!
It is sad and bad
Too bad

So sad

Dear Brothers and Sisters
Self-neglect as nations is but an unreasonable risk
This should not be your take
Cut those cuffs of bigotry
Think about a united Africa
Where Africans will be safe and free
Where Africans will work and walk free
Africa belongs to Africans
This is the meaning of the freedom you fought for
Please don't tarnish it
Please *Zumbe* show us the light

Bafowethu in Mpumalanga
Have you ever heard of Africans stranded in India?
They are called Jarawa
They are confined in the island of Andaman
They are treated like animals
Simply because they are not Indian

How come you are doing the same?
As if you are not of the same pedigree
Thixo we need your glee

Ironically and interestingly, while Africans are
discriminated against in India
The world has kept mum as if they are not human beings
Africa has maintained silence as if the Jarawa are not
Africans
Africa has failed to question this brutality and oddity
Indians enjoy Africa despite their haecceity
Again, how can Africa fight for others while it still needs
to be fought for?
Africa that has refused to reunite will always be vulnerable
A divided Africa will always be eaten and treated like any
perishable
This is the truth however horrible it jingles

Imbadla in Bulawayo
Lions do not discriminate against each other
Birds too don't commit such turpitude
They dearly and naturally love each other
Again, they are just beasts
How can humans act like imps?
Why are humans behaving like fish and snakes?
Fish and snakes eat each other depending on their sizes
What went wrong my brothers and sisters?
Afrophobia isn't a solution
Ambuye we need your salvation

Bazalwane in Kwazulu Natal
Hyenas don't habitually eat their colleagues
Despite being ravenous
The respect their blood
They honour their creed
They're but beasts indeed

Yet, they respect their lineages
Why acting like ogres
Especially, against your yesterday's compatriots
Chineke, send us chariots

Dear South African Brothers and Sisters
Is Afrophobia an answer?
Please, try to reason collectively
You will see it clearly
That, indeed, Afrophobia is but a bigger problem
It is a bigger problem than the one you encounter
Therefore, my brothers, sisters and friends
Please, use just common sense
You'll see the imminent danger of Afrophobia
Ambuye we seek your help against this self-destructive
mania

Bazalwane in Cape
Will Afriphobia give back your land?
Will it fight rampant corruption in the ranks?
Will it feed your progenies?
Will Afrophobia provide you houses or careers?
The answer is a big nope
If this is the case
Why then tarnish you image?
By committing such a sacrilege
Stop this imprudence
It won't do you well as state
Ewe Mulungu, give us sanity

Join me *umunne* in Nigeria
I call upon the government of South Africa
Please urgently enlighten your people
Tell them openly and kindly
That Afrophobia won't do them good
Instead, it will ruin the country for good

Neighbours will hate you
They'll shy away from you
Who knows what comes tomorrow?
If you face a problem that needs them
They will never come to your aid again
We need your guidance ancestors

Abale in Malawi
Affected countries should stand together
Let their ties with South Africa sever
Let them make their point clear
Afrophobia never
Let the powers that be see
How they've exacerbated the problem
The time they kept mum
They created mayhem
Now look at this bloodbath
We need leadership forthwith

Bakaulengwe in Botswana
No country is an island
Even islands need others
Nobody can live alone and function
Especially, for the nation
Cooperation is the only tool
That enhances the country to prosper
We need each other
Whether we like it or not
This is a natural reality
Who needs Afrophobia?
Who needs racism?
Perpetrated by the people of the same pedigree
Ancestors we need your glee
Barab' abo in Lesotho
Shame on Afrophobia
Shame on those perpetrating it

Shame on those who condone it
Shame
Shame
Shame
Ishe, save us from this shame

Did You Know?

Authorities have to stop this violence
For violence begets violence
This needs adhocracy
But not mediocracy
Neither does it need idiocy
Let's embark on policies
That will address the problems of the mass
Authorities need to take their place
Which is to address issues that citizenry faces
Mr. President please
Please rein in and get the country out of this mess
Look at your people in their eyes
Tell them that what they are doing is erroneous
Let them come back to their sense
Let's take on Afrophobia *en masse*
Africans should not become part of this madness
Madness against their brothers and sisters

Stop duetting with criminals that enacted apartheid
Stop a new form of apartheid even if it is African enacted
Apartheid is apartheid
There is no legal or good apartheid
Be it Afrophobic or based on hatred
Apartheid is apartheid
Stop monkey business; it is putrid and obnoxious
Stop; it won't bring you any good
We need your wisdom good Lord

Your Excellency Mr. President
I heard you talking of the BEE project
Yes, Black Economic Empowerment
Didn't it become Black Economic Embezzlement?
What is your assessment of it if we face it?

How many did BEE benefit in reality
What was in your deployment
Did you consider gender equality?
Was it done base on equity
How many poor South Africans got that empowerment?
Did you invite your associates?
How many *hoi polloi* did you pull out of poverty?
Was there any venality
In distributing financial and economic empowerment
Why we see millions in poverty
Where did BEE money go?

Seriously, take graft on
Graft in everything the authorities do wrongly
Embark on accountability intrepidly
Avoid self-help mentality that hasn't worked
Avoid nepotism and loyalty
Deliver people from poverty
Give them enhancement
Do everything transparently and rightly
Surely, equally, deliver justice to all inhabitants
Go back to the stipulations of the constitution
It provides clearly that all South African residents deserve
protection

Dear South Africans
Let me remind you kindly
Please, take this seriously
There are issues you agreed upon during your liberation
Do you remember what the issues were?
Remember how the hopes of the nation were
Well, land redistribution topped on the agendas
Those you promised the land think it was but propagandas
Landless South Africans need land
They can't produce without land
You've landless black majority

Landless in their state
Why don't you do something about it?
They need land to cultivate
They belong to it
It belongs to them
Land is one of things that defines humanity
Please give them their land

Land is more than the means of production
Land defines people; and to it they have connection
We are who we are because of our land
Our connection to our land is sacred
Without our land we are but naught
Without it, we collectively or individually are doomed
How come animals have land but not humans?
How come birds have nests but not humans?
How come bats have cages as their houses but not
humans?
To be truly humans depends on how we own our land
Yes, our completeness is on how we relate to our land
Therefore, we need our land back for our survival
All quacks and landgrabbers holding it must know this
Our land is nonnegotiable
Without it we are but everything ignoble

Dear Common Man and Woman
Let me help you my kin
Go ask for land and economic empowerment
Foreigners don't have any stake in your plight
It is only indifference and myopic indulgent
That force you to see things differently
Foreigners have nothing to do with your predicament
Try to seize this opportunity
Take on the authorities
Ask about your constitutional rights
Again, don't hate

Don't attack and persecute
Just stand on the line of right
This way, the world will give its support

Dear South Africans
We collectively need to put an end to blasphemy
We need to collectively declare that Afrophobia is but
infamy
It doesn't befit a nation
That calls itself a rainbow nation
Rainbow nation that shuns nations
Is it really a rainbow nation?
Or the nation of hammers and bows
Ishe, save us from these self-inflicted blows

Dear South African Brothers and Sisters
Killing or robbing others won't solve your problems
So, too, xenophobic attacks always create vengeance and
mayhem
The product of all this is nothing but national shame
Stop this crazy blame game
As sane people, go to the spirit of the problem
Yes, take on the real problem
To solve the problem, avoid farfetched pretexts
Realistically, get into the core of the matters
This way, every step you take, indeed, will have great
impacts
Never lose this opportunity
Please, seriously, stop this animosity cum insanity
Instead, embark on peaceful means
Sanity is the only civilised means
Stop and shun Afrophobia

What A Pity!

Dear Brothers and Sisters
Do you know the architects of apartheid?
I will give you their names
They are Abraham Kuiyper and Nico Diederichs,
Don't forget Piet Meyer, Geoff Cronje and Hendrik
Frensch Verwoerd
Others are Daniel François Malan and Jacob Daniel du
Tot
These are the criminals that enacted apartheid
Among many more
Equate them with the like of Cardinal Charles Lavigrie
This is a criminal who sowed the seed of Rwandan
genocide
Just like divide and rule of Africa for Lord Fredrick
Lugard
These are the criminals we still mindlessly hold dear
While these criminals are laughing in their graves
Rara avis like Nelson Mandela are crying in their graves
Solomon Mahlangu, Steve Biko and others are grieving in
their sepulchers
Why shouldn't they if at all you're battering their sacrifice
Why shouldn't they cry while you're creating such a mess?
Why shouldn't they if at all you're violating their wills?
Wills of togetherness and peace
The will of unity of Africans

Dear Brothers and Sisters
Imagine if it were you facing the killings by your kinships
What a pity at this juncture is?
Those criminals above are laughing in their sepulchers
They cachinnate and rejoice
Knowing that their victims and stooges
Have fulfilled their work of dehumanising Africans

This can't be your place
Otherwise, you are senseless
Please, stop this recklessness
Let's reunite Africa to its oneness
O *Ishe*, make us recompense

Do you know Brothers and sisters?
A fool is the one bitten twice
In the same hole
Apartheid bit you
Why doing it to others
Why repeating the same wickedness?
That saw you suffer despicable miseries
Ambuye, save us from chaos

What Africa has suffered is enough
Corruption and exploitation are enough
Why adding another catastrophe to the life that's been
already tough?
Based on Afrophobia not to mention scoff
What we've already suffered is enough
Enough is enough
Please dear brothers and sisters in the South
Don't add another melancholy
Yes, Afrophobia is
Mulungu, save us from this nadir
Hear our clangorous clamour
Restore our true African demeanour
So that we can reclaim our honour at this very hour
This is what I seek in any manner
I speak of the truly united Africa's future

Dear South Africans
I fully understand
When you ushered freedom
Everything was based on a new vision

The vision of a new democratic nation
You called it a rainbow nation
High was expectations
Now, over twenty years down the line
The majority still wallows in poverty
This isn't the vision
That the founding fathers envisioned
Let's put things back on truck
Let's face the real subjects
Abject poverty
Diseases
Forgetfulness
Landlessness
Graft
Ignorance
Insatiability
Selfishness
Etc. etc. etc.

The miseries Africa's already suffered are enough
Economic exploitation resulting from colonialism
Not to mention neo-colonialism
Not to mention imperialism
Now, we face this African-made racism
Please, this should be stopped
Afrophobia must be condemned
Those enacting should be charged
Let them serve their time for this crime
That's committed against humanity
The crime against oneself who discriminate against others
Mulungu hear our prayers

The world is laughing at us
All eyes are on us
Everything is laughing at us
Even beasts are laughing at us

Bemoaning and wondering
How can we act this senselessly?
They wonder about this mess
Whereby a person discriminates against self
We used to hear this in America and Asia
We heard in Canada and Australia
So, too, we heard about this in Europe
At home, we had confidence and hope
Racism was against Aborigine and Africans
Now, Africans are used it against Africans!
Nzambe, save our souls

When South Africa got its independence
The rays of euphoria and love emanated
Every African was happy
Saying "at last no African soil is still under colonialism"
Why turning such hope into euphemism?
Is this the South Africans mean by nationalism?
What type of nationalism?
That gives you heroism of committing crimes and
terrorism
No, this isn't nationalism
Call it whatever you want
This is but terrorism
Terrorism against innocent neighbours
Terrorism in the name of nationalism
Terrorism can't be nationalism
And nationalism can't be bolstered by terrorism
Ngai, save us from this chasm

I hear a bellow in me
It is excruciatingly bemoaning and unstoppably telling me
It tells me to tell you
What you are awkwardly doing is wrong
If anything, it is but a havoc
Soon you will become a laughingstock

Be warned, if you don't stop this lunacy
Other countries will shun you
And this will make your lives miserable
Don't take this direction
By all standards, it is evil and wrong
No way can I expressly explain it
I must be honest to you and myself and call a shovel a shovel
Afrophobia is sabotage
Those committing it should well know
Shikulu, please, send them a blow
All those who harm others

Where is the President?
He seems to have caught a cold foot
Why doesn't he urgently issue a writ?
For, doing so, I firmly believe, will stop this insanity
I, as well, call upon the parliament
I appealingly invoke the cabinet
Why are the members of parliament silent at this very moment?
While the country is on fire
Please, come out strongly and openly
Openly and seriously, condemn Afrophobia
Declare it a national calamity
Yes, it is indeed, a calamity of the mass in unfamiliarity
Please have it stopped instantly
Africa must be united to its entirety
Yes, unite against this vulgarity
BeNkosi, fiercely descend on this collective insanity
Save us from this boorish nationality
Save us from mass barbarity and brutality

Mr. President
Being the head of the executive
The world is waiting to hear your narrative

We seriously would like to evaluate every aspect of your
directive
We, too, want to know what you truly want to practically
achieve
By pliably keeping quiet on this mobocracy
You're promoting nothing but mass lunacy
Keeping mum takes away any sense of hagiocracy
Please, declare your stance as you maintain detectible
buoyancy
Come clean about this mess
Practically and urgently, deliver your people

Please Mr. President
Don't allow South Africa to go to the dogs
Please honorable parliament
Don't let South Africa become dirt like hogs
You are but custodians of justice
Palpably note that the history you are making today
The very history will stand forever for others to see
When this moment arrives, where will you put your faces?
Where will your faces be in this mockery
Presiding over an Afrophobic country
Instead of staying a side and look
Saying something will get you off the hook
You need to create works
Offer civil education to your society
So that citizens can see what they can't see currently
Teach them equality
They'll respect human dignity
Afrophobic attacks won't create any employment
So, too, it won't bring development
Neither shall it redistribute land
Embark on true empowerment
Stop Afrophobic onslaught
It is but a bomb that will kill them
Please *Modingwana*, guide those at the helm

South Africa is a young country
It needs to invest in sanity
Criminality breeds criminality
Chaos won't bring development
The country needs development
Africa needs development
It is only through solidarity
That we can reach the summit
Let's condemn venality
If we make this attempt
Our country will meet its target
The target of prosperity
The target of equality

Go back to the drawing board if you wish
Please do your homework as you avoid the whitewash
Condoning the crime makes your job wishy-washy
Look at what you agreed without any sway
The issues that you asked during struggle were land
Economic empowerment also featured high
Authorities should meet the prospects of the *hoi polloi*
By embarking on legal and constructive efforts of arresting
the problems
Afrophobia won't bring any respite
If it brings anything, it is nothing but bedlams
Afrophobia surely will ruin the state
God save South Africa from this insanity
Save it from Afrophobia and transgression
Safe Africa from itself

Please tell those haters
Cruelty is for beasts although not all beasts
Violence doesn't befit humans
Differently from beasts, humans are awarded with brains

What's stopping South African from collectively putting
the brains to use
If their collective sanity is used properly, they will solve
their problems
This must however be done in civilized manners
For whoever subscribes to it, hating is detrimental
For whoever employs it, torturing is criminal
The nation should not take such a venue of destruction
It will soon pay dearly
Do pray for clemency as a nation

Dear Brothers and Sisters
South Africa bigly needs to go back to reconciliation
Go back to the agreement of freedom
South Africa was promised land reformation
Why has it not been carried out then?
South Africans were promised of economic empowerment
Empowerment for all
Not just for a clique of friends and crawlers
South African leaders need to go back to the essentials
Instead of letting the country embark on self-destruction
We invoke God to avert this aberration

Dear BRETHREN
Africa needs forgiveness
We need to forgive each other and move forward
Shall this happen, avoid recidivism
Repeating the same sin means vengeance
If we truly forgive each other
We must do so as we heroically and truly face the future
Africa's future is in unity and purpose
Apply your Ubuntu philosophy
You are because I am

Dear Brothers and Sisters
I see no excuse for Afrophobia

It isn't a viable means but myopia
Let South Africans and all Africans know this
Macabre as it looks
Afrophobia is but a poisoned chalice
Nobody should drink from it
Nobody should defend it
Whoever sees it must break it
No nation should make do with it
Tolerating such a vice is but turning the nation into imps
Modimo, save us from these dips

Dear Brothers and Sisters
Who wants the nation of criminals?
The nation of brigands
Who wants it?
Tell me without any duplicity
Can criminality reward any humanity?
Isn't it insanity to embark on criminal acts?
How many'd we reproach to understand this fact?
Afrophobia is abomination
Especially for the whole nation of humans
The nation whose people hate other humans

Mungu Twaomba

Dear all I must say it clearly
I say it openly and loudly
As I seriously call upon our people to make a sacrifice
Invoke our demised Gods to help our continent
I know you know its misgivings and predicaments
Never waste time with colonial deities
We were perpetually colonised in their incongruous names
We lost our beautiful and rightful names in their names
We became mere weak and wicked things in their names

Go back to your roots and seek the intervention of our
ancestors
Those who put Africa together
Those who preserved everything for us now to destroy
today
Those who laid the foundations of our ways
Yes, those who always oversee on us as we deride their
good deeds

In the name of our ancestors and Gods
We raise our voices and hands
Hear us *Mungu* our *Modimo*
We pray for South Africa and Africa as well
Heed us as we shriek and yell *Thixo*
We seriously pray for sanguinity
We always pray for prosperity
The prosperity that all Africans will share with equity
From you we seek abundance and justice
Mungu banish dearth and injustices
We verily pray for solidarity
As we truthfully abhor criminality
Let us stand together and fight for our dignity
Let Africans fight for their unity

Let's fight for conviviality
As we abhor greed and inanity
Unkulukulu save our souls
Save us from ourselves
Restore our peace and tranquility

Let's say it in unison together
At the top of our lungs let's holler and holler
Committedly and determined let's make it clear
That Afrophobia isn't an answer to our problems
If it helps, it will exacerbate our problems
Let's stand together
Let's fight Afrophobia wherever it is
Let's utter it together without *cum grano salis*
Afrophobia never
Solidarity ever
Oneness of Africa ever
Unity of Africa forever
God grant us our desire
Save our brethren from Afrophobia
Let them shun Afrophobia
Let them see the light
Cure them from myopia

Mungu wetu twakuomba
Unkulunkulu siyakhuleka
Mwari twakunamata
Modimo rea rapela
Allah muna addu'a
Uthixo thina twakutandaza
Zumbe Muungu taakuombeza
Ngai twakuthaitha
We pray for your harmony
Save Africa from its self-perpetuated acrimony

Mungu ibariki Afrika

Wabariki watu wake
Zirejeshe tunu zake
Wazindue viongozi wao
Waone mwanga nao
Urejeshe utu wao
Waiunganishe Afrika

God bless Africa
Bless its peoples
Return its splendours
Awaken their leaders
So that they see the light
Resume their humanity
They reunite Africa

For, *utu wa mtu ni watu*
Yes, *ubuntu ngumuntu ngabantu*
True, *umuntu ngumuntu ngabantu*
A person is a person through other people

Ishe ropafadza iAfrika
Nkosi sikelel iAfrika
Maluphakanyisw' uphondo lwayo
Yizwa imithandazo yethu
Nkosi sikelela, thina lusapho lwayo
God bless Africa

Printed in the United States
by Baker & Taylor Publisher Services